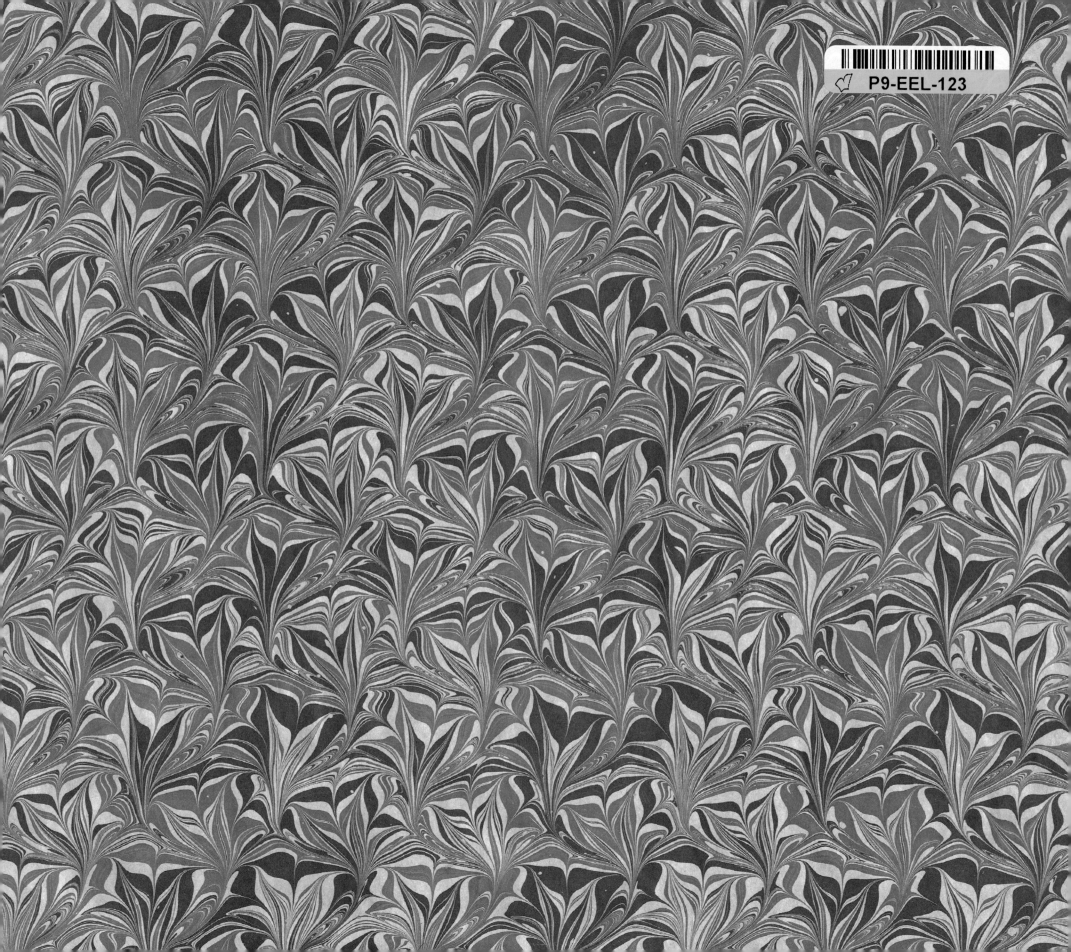

CALIFORNIA PASTORALE

Mission San Carlos Borromeo del Rio Carmelo, Carmel, Monterey County, c.1890.

FOR California is a poem! The land of romance,
of mystery, of worship, of beauty and Song.

Ina Coolbrith

Grazing sheep near Pasadena, Los Angeles County, 1906. A.C. Vroman, F. W. Martin Collection.

CALIFORNIA PASTORALE

Selected Photographs 1860-1925

Introduction by Gary F. Kurutz

Compiled by Windgate Press

WINDGATE PRESS : SAUSALITO, CALIFORNIA

Library of Congress Cataloging-in-publication Data

California pastorale : Selected photographs 1860— 1925 / introduction
   By Gary F. Kurutz ; compiled by Windgate Press.
         p.   cm.
      Includes index.
      ISBN 0-915269-12-0
      1. Landscape photography— California— History— 19th century.
      2. Landscape photography— California— History— 20th century.
      3. California— Pictorial works. I. Windgate Press.
   TR660.5.C35 1997
   799' .36794— dc21   97-48531
                                                             CIP

Typography and films by I.C.S. Spokane, Washington
Printed by Publishers Press, Salt Lake City, Utah
Designed by L. Witwer Bonnett

FIRST PRINTING

WINDGATE PRESS : SAUSALITO CALIFORNIA

Photographer Isaiah West Taber recording solar eclipse, Cloverdale, Sonoma County, 1889.

Washerwoman's Lagoon, San Francisco, 1858, Carleton Watkins.

INTRODUCTION

"A California Pastorale,
With simple rustic themes,
And ancient melodies recall
Deep from treasured dreams."

Anon., 1895

To early settlers, California's sublime beauty and unmatched geographic diversity provided a perfect subject for the artist, writer, and photographer. All combined to create an image that made the Golden State the envy of the nation. So successful was the image that it resulted in a population influx that has, for the most part, erased that picture of a tranquil, bucolic all-year land of "health, wealth, and sunshine."

Windgate Press for well over a decade has produced a series of elegant books fully demonstrating the power of historical photographs not only to document a particular subject or era but also to create an ambience that provokes and stimulates the eye of the viewer. *California Pastorale*, through the images they have so thoughtfully selected and arranged, depicts a seemingly rural and unspoiled California but one with a hint of human incursion and anticipation of change. Photographs such as these played a pivotal role in luring thousands and then millions of tourists and homeseekers to this land of golden sunsets, jagged coastlines, verdant rolling hills, lush orchards, and cathedral-like valleys.

The word *pastorale* evokes thoughts of uncomplicated rustic music and pastoral scenes. In terms of California's past, it recalls that halcyon time prior to the Gold Rush romanticized and popularized by the likes Helen Hunt Jackson and Gertrude Atherton and scores of other writers. It is a nostalgic period best recalling dashing dons, enchanting señoritas, jolly brown-robed friars, fandangos, fiestas, and the fragrance of orange blossoms. This Arcadian myth was a cornucopia of plenty with bountiful orchards, luxuriant gardens, and sprawling ranchos, and with its people living in the sunny, delicious, winterless California air. That image of California as Eden, as clearly demonstrated in this book, continued well into this century.

In the context of today's California and its population of 37 million, it is hard to believe that one hundred years ago almost the entire state was back country. Only San Francisco east of Van Ness Avenue gave any hint of mature development. Even Los Angeles at that time was primarily agricultural. Many of the rustic locales reproduced on these pages now host thousands of commercial and residential buildings intersected by concrete and asphalt roadways. Cahuenga Pass seen in 1890 (*page 106*) with its narrow dirt road, for example, gave way to one of the busiest traffic corridors in the world, the Hollywood Freeway. A modern commuter would hardly believe it. Tidy family farms would give way to agribusiness, high desert valleys would yield their water to populous basins, and general stores would evolve into shopping malls.

The image of California, of course, did not come from photographs alone. Artists such as Thomas Hill and Albert Bierstadt painted majestic scenes of California. They in turn gave way to the *plein air* painters and impressionists who saw in California's rural scenery a unique source of light, a land of eternal springtime. Many of these same artists such as Maynard Dixon, Maurice Logan, William Bull, and Arthur James Cahill received commissions to illustrate posters, books, magazines, promotional brochures, railroad time tables, and parade programs. The stunning color covers produced for these publications created a vision of California as paradise on earth, the perfect place to live.

Words served to further enhance and confirm what the visitor to California could expect to see. Nowhere is this better demonstrated than in Charles Nordoff's classic book, *California: For Heath, Pleasure, and Residence* (1872). A stream of other wordsmiths and their books followed.

Beneath the Palisades, Santa Monica, c.1890.

Weary photographer A.P. Hill, Menlo Park, San Mateo County, c.1895.

Benjamin C. Truman, hired by the Southern Pacific to promote its great resort hotel, the Del Monte; Charles Frederick Holder, founder of Pasadena's Rose Parade and author of dozens of books on outdoor recreation; Charles Francis Saunders, with his rhapsodic *Under the Sky in California*; J. Smeaton Chase, writing on California's coast, desert, and Yosemite trails; and Ernest Peixotto, to name just a few, created word pictures equal in power to the oil-on-canvas painter.

Magazines as well, embellished with illustrations and articles by the above named artists, writers and poets, contributed mightily to the promotion of California. *The Overland Monthly*, *Sunset*, *The Land of Sunshine*, and *California's Magazine* all featured articles with tempting advertisements extolling California's natural features and its unlimited opportunity. Automobile associations, as evidenced by early issues of *Touring Topics* and *Motorland*, gave the pre-freeway motorist ideas as to where to go for easy-to-reach weekend and vacation excursions.

A subgroup of this literature of praise and wonder consisted of the brochures and booklets printed by the thousands to lure tourists and settlers to a sparsely populated California. Seemingly every city and county issued a publication touting its boundless opportunity, low cost of living, unexcelled weather, and unlimited water supply. Land-rich railroads, with Southern Pacific leading the way, also turned out these eye-catching publications in great number.

Many of these books, magazines, and promotional brochures relied heavily on photography to bolster their florid text and convince the reader of the reality of this modern Eden. Photographs of grazing livestock, fruit trees in blossom, broad wheat fields, irrigation canals, handsome farms and ranches, wholesome towns, stately hotels, breathtaking natural wonders, picnics on the beach, missions and adobe ruins, and roads lined with palm trees and eucalyptus no doubt had a potent effect on the would-be tourist or potential Californian. The photography captions for a brochure called *Sunny Southern California*, for example, demonstrate the linkage between words and images: "The crumbling missions recall glories of other days," "A perpetual fairyland of fragrant blooms," "The intriguing call of the beaches is ever heard," and "From city boulevards to groves of golden fruit." Photography possessed a unique power as a reliable witness and the booster took full advantage of that medium.

Recognizing this marriage of words and photographs, Windgate Press has skillfully drawn upon the vast body of California descriptive and travel literature. The juxtaposition of poignant contemporary quotations with photographs serves to amplify the lyrical qualities of this rustic, wide open land of Canaan.

As suggested by this book, the photographic record of that growth-oriented era shows an idealized California devoid of social strife, environmental exploitation, mismanagement of natural resources, and

Emerald Bay, Lake Tahoe, El Dorado County, c.1910, Frederick Martin.

Amateur photographers, c.1900.

overcrowding. It was a different era with different values. As Susan Landauer points out in her insightful essay in *California Impressionists*, "the Californians [painters] portrayed a world in which humanity lived in harmonious intimacy with the land." The *plein air* painters longed for an uncorrupted, pre-industrial California. Indirectly, the same may be said of the photographers whose work is reproduced in *California Pastorale*. Here man and nature seemed to coexist in peace.

California photographers of the nineteenth and early part of this century made a living by commissions or by selling pleasing or interesting views. Photography was a tool used to further the goals and desires of the client. Businesses and boards of trade hired photographers to demonstrate industrial progress and opportunity; homeseeker bureaus and chambers of commerce utilized city and town views to prove that California was a civilized, safe place; tourist associations sent scores of photographers into the field to capture the grandeur of the state's natural diversity and resorts; and individuals commissioned photographers to record their likenesses and their homes or estates. Photographers with an artistic bent went off to the Yosemite Valley, Lake Tahoe, and other attractive locales, made up albums and boxed sets of selected scenic views for sale to tourists, the well-to-do, and any others who visited their viewing rooms.

With the advent of lighter cameras, dry plate and then flexible film negatives in the 1890s, photography became less arcane and less costly.

Interest in the craft exploded as amateur photography came into its own. Family photograph albums evolved from expensive elegantly bound volumes of portraits taken by a professional in the confines of a salon to economical cloth bindings encasing sheets of black paper holding snapshots taken by family members and friends of cheerful events such as children playing, weddings, and vacation trips. Others took up photography as a serious hobby, joined camera clubs, and went off into the California countryside hoping to create images of visual merit. Just like the hobbyist painter with his or her box of oil paints, brushes, and canvases, the amateur photographer more often than not chose rural subjects: trees, fields of wild flowers, the coastline, deserted adobes, and desert canyons.

Photographers of this bygone time captured the flavor of California without its bite. Like *plein air* oil painting, photographs portrayed an idyllic landscape all but devoid of human activity. Views of slums, strikes, ramshackle dwellings of migrant farm workers, warships spilling oil into the bay, or factories spewing toxic fumes were not the type of situations or subjects that Californians in general recognized or wanted to buy or commission.

The photographs presented here are from the files and shelves of the California History Section of the California State Library in Sacramento. Library staff obtained these pictures over many years with the view of documenting California's varied past. Many photos formed part of a family

9

Tehachapi Loop, Southern Pacific Railroad, Kern County, c.1880, Carleton Watkins.

Inglewood, Los Angeles County, c.1885, I. W. Taber.

or business archive, others came from the acquisition of a photographer's collection, and still others were added to the collection image by image. They reflect, though, what has survived and what individuals of times past deemed important.

A regional photography collection like that of the State Library typically focuses on cities and towns, fairs and expositions, parades, agriculture, natural wonders and disasters, industry, transportation, tourist attractions, historic landmarks, and people. These images also reflect various photographic technologies ranging from dramatic 16 x 20 inch albumen mammoth plate photographs from the 1870s to tiny snapshots from the 1920s. They also show a range of styles and interests reflecting the reality of picture taking before the camera became a standard household item.

Professional photographers, with an artistic flair and a sense of the region's unique landscape, produced the vast majority of images reproduced in *California Pastorale*. Chronologically, this visual essay begins with the brilliant albumen prints of Carleton E. Watkins from the 1870s and 1880s and concludes in the 1920s with the F. W. Martin Collection of landscapes and landscape architecture. Photographs by I. W. Taber of San Francisco, C. W. J. Johnson of Monterey, O. V. Lange of San Francisco and Berkeley, and William Fletcher of Los Angeles likewise produced images that both inform and delight. Others, while high in quality, lack a photographer's imprint or signature suggesting the hand of a skilled amateur.

While this book is not intended to serve as a history of California photography or a survey of all photographers who made pastoral images, it is worth identifying more fully some of the above named creators of these comely views. Carleton E. Watkins reigns as California's premier pioneer photographer and needs no introduction. His mammoth plate views of Yosemite and the Big Trees called international attention to California, and in recent years, historians, art historians, publishers, and museums have celebrated his magnificent work. The Library obtained an impressive selection of the master's mammoth plates, albums, and stereographs in the 1890s through the assistance of Watkins' friend and biographer, Charles B. Turrill. The Library at the time recognized the importance of Watkins and actively sought to build a collection of his work.

The quality of Watkins' photographs is unsurpassed and it is no accident that he dominates the pages of *California Pastorale*. Included is a striking three-part panorama of the great Yosemite Valley (*pages 42–43*). While his images of this unparalleled natural wonder brought Watkins recognition, he provided an invaluable service by lugging his cameras and glass plates up and down the Pacific slope capturing California on the eve of its urban growth. His prints of the nascent University of California from the Berkeley hills, Washerwoman's Lagoon in San Francisco, the California missions in ruins, and the dock of the Pacific Coast Steamship Company at San Diego transformed the prosaic into the picturesque.

Vacationers near Pacific Grove, Monterey County, c.1880.

COME SIT beside me on the sand,
and far across the sea
Where sunset paints the wings of night,
we'll dream of a day to be.

Percy A. Montgomery, 1911

Echo Park, Los Angeles, c.1890, William Fletcher.

Monrovia, Los Angeles County, c.1890, William Fletcher.

Often overlooked in creating the visual record of the Golden State are the scenic views of Watkins' commercial rival, Isaiah West Taber. From his elegant photographic parlors on San Francisco's Post Street, Taber orchestrated a pictorial business unmatched on the Pacific Coast. Like a captain of industry, he sent anonymous photographers out into the field, obtained the negatives of others, and photographed celebrities visiting San Francisco. From this vast pictorial reservoir, he marketed multiple albums of picturesque views such as *Photographic Album of Principal Business Houses, Residences, and Persons* (1880), *California Scenery & Industries* (1884) and sold thousands of individual prints. The Ingelwood irrigation ditch and Hotel Raymond in South Pasadena demonstrate the quality of images that bear his imprint. As with Watkins, the 1906 San Francisco Earthquake and Fire destroyed his negative collection.

The opening of Southern Pacific's plush new Monterey Peninsula resort, the Hotel del Monte in 1880, gave photographer Charles Wallace Jacob Johnson a fabulous opportunity. Earning a spot as the hotel's photographer, he systematically recorded its buildings, grounds and guests. When not printing glass negatives from his resort studio, he traversed the sublime Monterey countryside and coastline with his 5 x 7 inch camera making scores of images that would convince anyone that his region offered a siren-like blend of natural beauty and manmade elegance. Johnson's cabinet size prints of Ocean Avenue in Carmel (*page 90*),

bicyclers in their Victorian attire on the beach, and the windswept Monterey Cypress portray scenes uniquely Californian.

Oscar Voss Lange of San Francisco produced a remarkable series of views of the San Mateo Peninsula in the early 1880s. His 10 x 13½ inch albumen prints exemplify pastoral California. The peninsula with its verdant hillsides, towering redwoods, and aromatic groves of eucalyptus proved irresistible to a photographer of his skill. But as Lange recorded, this woodland, located in close proximity to the teeming metropolis of San Francisco, attracted the city's elite, and soon, monuments to American enterprise in the form of sprawling estates interrupted forever the peninsula's sylvan landscape. Lange eventually left San Francisco for the hills of Berkeley and won acclaim for his images of the growing University of California.

William Fletcher, a resident of Los Angeles' first suburb, Angelino Heights, provided graphic evidence of what that evangelical writer Benjamin Truman called "Semi-Tropical California." If ever a photographer gave credence to the writings of the booster, it was William Fletcher. His work received little recognition until the Library obtained a major group of his glass negatives, cabinet cards, and stereo views in 1984. For the first time, his work could be studied as a whole rather than as isolated images. Like so many others from that boomer era, Fletcher was not a native Californian. He left Vermont for sunny Los Angeles in 1885 and established a

The Golden Gate, San Francisco Bay, c.1885, I.W. Taber.

Frederick W. Martin, c.1908.

photographic business. No longer having to contend with winter snows, he was free to roam the idyllic countryside of his adopted home. His views of near empty San Fernando, Verdugo and San Gabriel valleys; the fledgling towns of Pasadena, San Gabriel, and Monrovia; new homes surrounded by freshly planted palms, pampas grass, and citrus orchards; and the beaches at Redondo and Santa Monica embodied the California dream.

One collection, perhaps more than any other, gave inspiration to this book. The acquisition of the glass and film negatives and albums of the Frederick W. Martin Studio of Pasadena in 1994 brought into the Library an extraordinary collection of public and residential architecture primarily covering the years 1910 to 1925. Thousands of views of pergolas, patios, fountains, reflecting pools, eucalyptus groves, fields of wild flowers, palm lined streets, missions, and coastal roads gave proof that somehow man-made and natural environments could coexist. Some of his meticulously composed photographs show newly-built mansions that look as though they had been dropped into the virgin valleys of California without disturbing the topography or vegetation.

Albums of professional views provide a key contribution to depicting rustic California. Joseph Spencer Cone of Marietta, Ohio, moved to California during the Gold Rush and, in 1869, bought Rancho Rio de los Berrendos on the east bank of Sacramento River near Red Bluff, Tehama County. Cone commissioned a photographer whose name eludes us to record his 14,000 acre domain of irrigation canals, wheat fields, orchards, and livestock. The skillful photographer created from this common ranch setting a surprising beautiful pictorial work. Sunlit haystacks, grazing sheep, and cows crossing a stream appear frozen in time ready to be captured by the painter. A six-part panorama of a leaf-carpeted oak forest and a photographer standing next to his dry plate camera is breathtaking for its intuitive sense of composition and use of light.

Another album represented in this book consists of 144 images depicting the Owens Valley before its encounter with water seekers from Los Angeles. Dating from around 1905, it preserves a view of the valley when agriculture and livestock dominated. Andrew Forbes who operated a photographic studio in Bishop from 1903 to 1916 took many of the images found in the album. This thick, oblong volume gives visual evidence of an Owens Valley immortalized in Mary Austin's California classic, *The Land of Little Rain*.

Many other views by known and unknown photographers grace the pages of *California Pastorale*. Some will beguile, others will invoke a sense of nostalgia for a simple California of long ago, and others will produce startling feelings of disbelief as to how much the landscape has changed. Each, however, will reward the viewer with the photographer's acumen.

Gary F. Kurutz
Sacramento, August 1997

C ALIFORNIANS are people who were born
somewhere else and then came to their senses.

Will Rogers

Above, Millbrae, home of Darius Ogden Mills, San Mateo County, c.1880, Carleton Watkins.
Left, Californians in Tehama County, c.1898.

CALIFORNIA is a land of purple shadows and
blue skies. The gold of the hillside, the blue of the ocean,
produce unpainted pictures in lavish abundance.
Wild flowers—unwritten poems—greet you everywhere.

William Greer Harrison, 1904

Above, meadow and Mt. San Gorgonio, San Bernardino County, 1922, Frederick Martin.
Left, San Fernando Valley, Los Angeles County, 1909, Frederick Martin.

G O WHERE we will on the surface of things,
men have been there before us.

Henry David Thoreau, 1849

Above, graveyard at Mission San Luis Rey de España, 1909, Frederick Martin.
Left, adobe ruin near Salinas, Monterey County, c.1900.

I F EVER California becomes a prosperous country,
this bay will be the center of its prosperity.

Richard Henry Dana, 1835

Above, Vallejo, Solano County, c.1878, Carleton Watkins.
Left, Golden Gate from Black Point, San Francisco, c.1870, Carleton Watkins.

DR. BUSHNELL was here in 1856. The College Trustees wanted the Doctor's help [in finding a suitable campus location], so I went with him all around the bay. San Mateo, Santa Clara, San Jose, New Almaden, Mission San Jose, Sunol's Valley, near Pleasanton—that was the Doctor's paradise! Water, landscape, retirement, and all. But then no railroad was projected in the state, and that site was too far off without a railroad.

Well, we were greatly taken with Brooklyn [Oakland], but how to get water up there! And then it was windy. We found Berkeley's climate better than we had thought. On the whole it seemed to combine more attractions than any other place. And so, April 16, 1860, the trustees held a formal meeting there, on and around a rock near the old road, and made choice of the site, invoking Heaven's blessing.

Daniel C. Gilman, President of the University of California, 1873

Above, University of California, North and South Halls, Berkeley, Alameda County, c.1880, Carleton Watkins.
Left, rose garden, Underhill Estate, Pasadena, 1913, Frederick Martin.

COME and range the uplands that front the western sea,
Where petrel's cry is mingled with landbird's melody;
Where silver-crested breakers, uptossed upon the strand,
Shout to the grassy billows that scud the meadow-land.

Leon J. Richardson, 1909

Above, Torrey Pines, San Diego County, 1919, Frederick Martin.
Left, Cypress trees, Seventeen-Mile Drive, Monterey County, 1919, Frederick Martin.

THE ANGELUS

Bells of the Past, whose long-forgotten music
Still fills the wide expanse,
Tinging the sober twilight of the Present
With color of romance!

Bret Harte, 1902

Above, Mission San Fernando Rey de España, Los Angeles County, 1890, A.C. Vroman, F. W. Martin Collection.
Left, bells of Mission San Juan Capistrano, Orange County, c.1908, Frederick Martin

THE MISSION buildings at San Juan Capistrano stand at the extreme edge of the village. Originally they consisted of an imposing belfried church adjoining an ample cloistered quadrangle. Today all of this is a ruin as has no counterpart this side of Italy, a ruin that artists love, and, no less, Nature. Upon the crumbling walls she has laid a tender hand.

Charles Francis Saunders, 1907

Above, Ruins of Mission San Juan Capistrano, c.1890, I.W. Taber
Left, ruins of church, Mission San Juan Capistrano, Orange County, 1908, Frederick Martin

VOICES in this land tell of many things, of adventure and promise, of noble work and triumph; they whisper the names of those who lived and loved. Another voice yet beckons all who hear the distant music: California!

Charles Held, 1908

Above, home of General John C. Frémont, Bear Valley, Mariposa County, c.1880, Carleton Watkins.
Left, Sutter's Fort, Sacramento, Sacramento County, 1888.

CAMPING IN YOSEMITE, 1900

Go by rail and stage; do not hire a team of animals. Send up supplies by slow freight four weeks in advance. Upon entering Yosemite at noon, it is well to lunch at the hotel, then visit the guardian's office to see if the freight consigned to his care has arrived safely. Here one can ask about hiring a team to haul the goods to a good camping ground. I can suggest a place not much infested by the madding crowd, and yet near the hotel; a grassy flat covered with young pines and cottonwoods near what is called "The New Middle Road."

Sunset, 1900

Above, Yosemite Valley, 1908, Frederick Martin.
Left, campsite in Yosemite Valley, c.1885.

IMAGINE yourself upon the top of Sierra Buttes, a mountain near the center of the Sierra County, lifting its double crown of pinnacled peaks high above the rest. A bewildering array of snowy peaks, of domes and crags and tree-feathered crests, of gulches and canyons and ravines, boiling foam-flecked streams and the gleaming waters of forest-girt lakes, everywhere meets your gaze.

Bourdon Wilson, 1910

Above, Young America Mine, Sierra Buttes and Lower Sardine Lake, Sierra County, c.1890.
Left, Sierra Buttes, Sierra County, c.1885.

G. H. Schubert,
LAPORTE, CAL.

Does it snow in California, you ask. Yes indeed. Like most everything in California, the snow is superlative. It is deeper, colder, and more beautiful than any I have yet encountered. The snow lies all year on Mount Lola. On July 21st I needed to go less than half a mile for snow to cool a big luscious watermelon.

Lyman Ogden, 1882

Above, Bellevue Mine near La Porte, Plumas County, 1903, G.H. Schubert.
Left, children on Gibsonville Ridge, Plumas County, 1903, G.H. Schubert.

M AN SEEMS to think that the trees were made for man. The truth is man was made for the trees. The trees came in the order of creation on the third day, while man was left to the very last. Man was never thought of until long after the trees were in full glory.

There is nothing plainer in all the pages of the Bible than the truth, that man was made to tend and keep the trees. There is nothing truer in all the pages of history than that where man destroyed the trees, he himself has been destroyed.

Joaquin Miller, 1900

Above, road in Yosemite Valley, 1908, Frederick Martin.
Left, trees in Sequoia National Park, Tulare County, 1919. Frederick Martin.

W hy shouldn't the air be pure and fine?

It is the same the angels breathe.

Mark Twain at Lake Tahoe

Above, Storm over Lake Tahoe, c.1876, Carleton Watkins.
Left, South Lake Tahoe and Mount Tallac, El Dorado County, c.1876, Carleton Watkins.

THIS is the one day of my life, and one that I will
always remember with pleasure. Just think of where I was.
Up there amid the pines and silver firs in the Sierran solitude,
in a snowstorm too and without a tent, I passed one of
the most pleasant nights of my life.

President Theodore Roosevelt, Yosemite, 1903

Left, The Domes from Sentinel Dome; center, Lyell Group; right Merced Group, Yosemite, c.1878–1881, Carleton Watkins.

WANDER a whole summer if you can. Thousands of God's wild blessings will search you and soak you as if you were a sponge and the big days will go by uncounted. If you are business tangled and so burdened by duty that only weeks can be got out of the heavy-laden year, give a month at least. The time will not be taken from your sum of life. Instead of shortening, it will indefinitely lengthen it and make you truly immortal. Nevermore will time seem short or long and cares will never again fall heavily on you, but gently and kindly as gifts from heaven.

John Muir, 1912

Above, Hughes Lake, Los Angeles County, 1924, Frederick Martin.
Left, mountain stream, Sequoia National Park, Tulare County, 1919, Frederick Martin.

Beneath the blue pavilion of the sky
I watch the summer pageantry drift by.
Miraculous beauty, green and gold and gray
And silence the one trumpet through the day.

O lavish loveliness, and velvet hours,
Stay with me longer than your opulent flowers:
But if you must depart, leave behind
Your memory when I am winter blind.

Charles Hanson Towne, 1910

Above, Sycamores on Baldwin's Ranch, San Bernardino County, 1919, Frederick Martin.
Left, Professor William F. Jackson and art students, Sacramento County, c.1886.

COMPARED to the sea itself its shores are modern, but compared with anything else, some of them reach back to a credible antiquity. The seashore is always there, and that the sands shift and the rocks submit, however reluctantly, to the persuasion of the ages, doesn't greatly affect the proposition. For eons uncounted there has been that irregular line about continents where land meets water. Beyond any plausible doubt it will last our time, and I am glad to believe it will, for there is no part of the land that is more indispensable to the satisfaction of us who dwell on it than its edges.

E.S. Martin, 1905

Above, Point Loma from Coronado, San Diego County, 1919, Frederick Martin.
Left, Bolinas Bay, c.1895, Marin County.

THE SEA is full of wandering foam,
The sky of driving cloud;
My restless thoughts among them roam...
The night is dark and loud.

Where are the hours that came to me
So beautiful and bright?
A wild wind shakes the wilder sea...
O' dark and loud's the night!

William Ernest Henley, 1876

Above, Mendocino, Mendocino County, c.1885, Carleton Watkins.
Left, Point Arena lighthouse, Mendocino County, c.1900.

Looking over its expanse, one is tempted to imagine that
California is a paradise suspended between heaven and earth for the
use of happy mortals that have attained to a perfect innocence and a
perfect peace. Truly, we who live continually in California, hardly
appreciate her extraordinary beauty.

Caroline Le Conte, 1910

Above, Indiana Colony, forerunner of Pasadena, Los Angeles County, c.1878, Carleton Watkins.
Left, Millbrae, San Mateo County, c.1880, Carleton Watkins.

THE ROAD runs past cultivated lands, through a forest of mimosa, over a bridge which spans an irrigation ditch, slowly climbing all the time past a spot known as the Garden of Eden, where oranges and lemons and apricots and figs and grapes assume gigantic proportions. The road becomes steep. It is slowly eating its way into the mountain, into the canyon famous for its palms. Then the old road climbs a mountain and descends abruptly into the Valley of Palms.

August, 1900

Above, lupines in bloom, Mint Canyon, Los Angeles County, 1922, Frederick Martin.
Left, Palm Canyon near Palm Springs, Riverside County, 1924, Frederick Martin.

THis grand show is eternal. It is always sunrise somewhere; the dew is never all dried at once; a shower is forever falling; vapor is ever rising. Eternal sunrise, eternal sunset, eternal dawn and gloaming, on sea and continents and islands, each in its turn, as the round earth rolls.

John Muir, c.1912

Above and left, desert and Mt. San Jacinto, Riverside County, 1922, Frederick Martin.

The Belmont Hotel, above, stood in Los Angeles at the corner of Temple Street and Belmont Street, about a mile and a half from the city's original plaza. The view from its observation tower presented this spectacular panorama of an unpopulated city looking generally northwest to the Hollywood Hills and, at far right, Cahuenga Pass. In the far-left distance is Santa Monica and the Pacific Ocean. In the right center distance is the bold form of Mt. Lee, site of today's famous Hollywood sign. Echo Park is hidden in the dark clump of trees several blocks from the hotel at right center. The new homes at right are part of Angelino Heights.

Overleaf, Los Angeles panorama.

Los Angeles, looking toward Hollywood from roof of Belmont Hotel, c.1889, William Fletcher.

IF ANYWHERE in the world one hears the call of the country clearly and sympathetically, it is in this delectable region where the farm has become the orange grove, and where one does not need to read a handbook on "How to Tell the Crops from the Weeds."

A. J. Wells, 1910

Verdugo Valley from Eysian Park, Los Angeles County, 1894, William Fletcher.

I CAME to California expecting a miracle.
Finding none, I made my own.

Anonymous, 1878

Above, farm in Monterey County, c.1880.
Left, San Jose home of D.L. Watson and family, Santa Clara County, c.1888.

2532 Mission St. S. F.
(over.)

Cottom, Artist.

Above, Robert Miller residence near Geyserville, Sonoma County, c.1885.

Every season in this new place we thank
the fates that brought us here.
Although we miss our friends back East,
California is our home.

Anonymous, 1878

Boathouse, Sonoma County, c.1900.

H OW WILL it be if there we find no traces—
There in Golden Heaven—if we find
No memories of the old Earth left behind,
No visions of familiar forms and faces
Reminders of old voices and old places?
Yet could we bear it if it should remind?

Edwin Markham, 1911

Above, harvesting alfalfa, Colusa County, c.1904.
Left, hardware store, St. Helena, Sonoma County, c.1890.

T HE VALLEYS of northern California bear some Spanish names as Pacheco, Ignacio, San Ramon, Rodeo, San Pablo and Pinole, but there are no longhorned cattle here. It is a peaceful countryside, a land of farms and farmers, with quiet towns not yet too ambitious to become cities.

A.J. Wells, 1910

Above, Andrew Smith residence, San Mateo County, c.1888, O.V. Lange.
Left, Muscat grapes, Tranquility Colony, Fresno County, c.1905.

CALIFORNIA's coastline is blessed with snug anchorages and grand
harbors where even the dullest of visionaries could foresee great cities.
From Drake and Cabrillo to the goldseekers of 1849, California's
sparkling coast has conjured up dreams of glory.

Etta Cary Ide, 1902

Above, Avalon, Catalina Island, Los Angeles County, c.1889, J.H. White.
Left, Pacific Coast Steamship Company wharf, San Diego, c.1878, Carleton Watkins.

In ACCORDANCE with predictions made in the early part of the season by well-informed eastern railway men, California is flooded with visitors. Never in the history of travel have there been so many health and pleasure seekers moved so great a distance in so short a time.

George H. Daniels, 1902

Above, Southern Pacific Railroad, San Fernando Tunnel and Andrews Station, Los Angeles County, c.1880, Carleton Watkins.
Left, Los Angeles and Independence Railroad depot, San Pedro Street, Los Angeles, c.1880, Carleton Watkins.

RAILROAD depots have a way of reminding you how far
you have come or how far yet you have to go. They ask an unspoken
question: Is this your final stop or will you move on? Californians
and railroad depots have a lot in common.

Charles Held, 1911

Above, North Pacific Coast Railway station at Red Hill, San Anselmo, Marin County, c.1895.
Left, Santa Fe Railroad depot, San Juan Capistrano, Orange County, c.1898.

71

Above, Second Street from Bunker Hill, Los Angeles, c.1900, I.W. Taber.

Los angeles

Gee, but this is a cheerful place,
A welcome smile on every face,
A hand that stretches out halfway
To help to pass the time of day.

Somehow this place has got a charm
That makes me want to sell the farm
Back East and settle down right here
Where things is full of warmth and cheer.

Henry F. Gilhofer, 1911

Griffith Park from Ivanhoe Street, Los Angeles County, 1886, William F. Fletcher.

ENJOY the "Grand Round," a spectacular carriage ride from Los Angeles through the finest agricultural region in the state. View the magnificent orange groves from the Hotel Raymond in South Pasadena, then on to the foothills and the Sierra Madre Villa, where a lavish table presents local wild game.

Advertising Circular, 1890

Above, Sierra Madre Villa, Los Angeles County, c.1880, Carleton Watkins.
Left, Hotel Raymond, South Pasadena, Los Angeles County, c.1890, I.W. Taber.

B ETWEEN Los Angeles and Ventura we had an opportunity
to see one of the most flourishing agricultural regions in the state.
Were it not for the bean fields of Ventura County, nearly the whole
of whose enormous yield is shipped to Boston, the people of that
city would be compelled to go beanless to bed.

E. Alexander Powell, 1914

Above, Hollywood, looking east from mouth of Laurel Canyon, Los Angeles County, c.1900, C.C. Pierce.
Left, tomato vines, West Hollywood near Sunset Boulevard, Los Angeles County, c.1900.

IN SAN DIEGO Country there is a little village called *El Nido,* the nest. On the map it is named otherwise, but to me it is always El Nido; for like the nest of a seagull, it is built on the edge of the cliffs, and the waves roll and crash against the rocks beneath it all day and throughout the night. The ordinary tourist comes seldom to the village; and when he does, its is with an air of expecting little. With the surge of the waves in his ears, he climbs down the steep side of the rock and stands on the gray stone shelves that barely escape the water at high tide. No one knows why he stays at El Nido; no one can tell you why he postpones his departure from day to day. Perhaps the sea could tell, but the sea hides well its secrets.

John Bruce MacCallum, 1904

Above, caves at La Jolla, (El Nido), San Diego County, 1910, Frederick Martin.
Left, old ranch near Mission San Diego, San Diego County, c.1880.

Soft as an echo of song
        Is the word which they whisper to me,
The wind that blows over the grass,
        The wind that blows in from the sea.

Ina Coolbrith, 1904

Above fisherman's cove near Redondo Beach, Los Angeles County, c.1895.
Left, Palisades near Santa Monica Canyon, Los Angeles County, c.1913, Frederick Martin.

PATRIOTIC Riverside residents are convinced that the nation needs one more holiday. Their representatives in the Legislature are behind a bill to make March 1st a State Orange Day, and their pro-motional bureau clamors for a national orange orgy. They would make it the duty of every one of the nation's millions to dispose of at least one orange on this day.

Editorial, Sunset Magazine, 1907

Above, Riverside citrus groves, c.1885.
Left, orange grove, Butte County, 1910.

O, SUNLIT land! Is it thy hidden wealth
Within the golden heart of rolling hills;
Or glint of gold across thy yellow poppy fields,
Or lingering rays of golden sun or serried peaks,
Ere yet it sinks into thy western seas,
That hither woos the wanderer's restless feet?

Josephine Mildred Blanch, 1907

Above, Sacramento River, c.1920.
Left, wheatfield, Sacramento County, c.1904, McCurry.

THOUGH actually the work of man, roads have long since come to seem so much a part of nature that we have grown to think of them as a feature of the landscape no less natural than rocks and trees. Nature has adopted them among her own works. [Roads] have for us a strange spiritual suggestiveness, so the vanishing road has gained a meaning beyond its use as the avenue of mortal wayfaring, and some roads indeed seem so lonely and so beautiful in their loneliness, that one feels the were meant to be traveled only by the soul.

Richard Le Gallienne, 1913

Above, Libby Estate, Ojai Valley, Ventura County, 1920. Frederick Martin.
Left, Pauma Ranch, Owens Valley, Inyo County, c.1900.

A DISTINCTIVE crop of the Golden State is the tourist, who blossoms in the sunlight of California into health and happiness. This great and precious crop has to be gathered and housed just as carefully and far more sumptuously than all the golden fruit and grain that is gathered into barns. California has learned how to build for all its crops but, in California, the proper housing of tourists has been advanced to a fine art.

A. J. Wells, 1910

Above, Archie on the hotel grounds, Del Monte Hotel, Monterey County, c.1885, C.W.J. Johnson.
Left, Del Monte Hotel, Monterey, Monterey County. C.1885, C.W.J. Johnson.

SOME FOLKS boast of quail on toast,
Because they think it's tony;
But I'm content to owe my rent,
And live on abalone.

By Carmel Bay, the people say,
We feed the lazzaroni
On Boston beans and fresh sardines
An toothsome Abalone.

Attributed to George Sterling and friends at Carmel, c.1898

Above, Point Lobos, Monterey County, 1900, Frederick Martin.
Left, Ocean Avenue looking west and Carmelo Hotel, Carmel, Monterey County, 1890, C.W.J. Johnson.

THE FIRST home we knew on this beautiful earth,
The friends of our childhood, the place of our birth,
In the heart's inner chamber sung always will be,
As the shell ever sings of its home in the sea!

Francis Dana Gage, 1880

Above, Sea Beach Hotel, Santa Cruz, Santa Cruz County, c.1890.
Left, Soquel Creek, Capitola, Santa Cruz County, c.1890.

THERE IS a little home in a quiet spot
Where the hosts of the sunlight rally,
Where trouble and care are both forgot
And worry's a specter that cometh not—
In Santa Clara Valley.

Anonymous, 1904

Above, Elk Horn Station, Paicines, San Benito County, c.1912, Britain.
Left, prune and apricot blossoms, Saratoga, Santa Clara County, c.1912, Lothers and Young Studios.

Hᴏᴡ ʜᴀʀᴅ to realize that every camp of men or beast has this glorious starry firmament for a roof! In such places standing alone on the mountaintop it is easy to realize that whatever special nests we make—leaves and moss like the marmots and birds, or tents or piled stone— we all dwell in a house of one room—the world with the firmament for its roof—and are sailing the celestial spaces without leaving any track.

John Muir

Above, Alvinza Hayward residence, San Mateo County, c.1885, O.V. Lange.
Left, Tranquillity Colony, Fresno County, c.1904.

THE WOODS are never silent. In the hush
   Of the high places solemnly there goes,
In endless undertone, the stately rush
   Of music—windy melody that grows,
And ebbs, and changes, in uncertain time:
   As if some pensive god tried here apart
Vague snatches of the harmonies sublime,
   Before he played them on the human heart.

Warren Cheney, 1901

Overleaf, Cone Ranch panorama.

Cone Oak Grove Ranch, near Red Bluff, Tehama County, c.1905.

HELLO, you little unexpected, curving, country road,
You look as though you might, perchance, lead on to Joy's abode!
What is there just beyond the turn down by that redwood tree?
You will not tell? O, very well, I'll just walk down and see!

Clarence Urmy, 1914

Neumann's Store, Woodside, San Mateo County, c.1885, O.V. Lange

WHAT does he plant who plants a tree?
A scion full of potency;
He plants his faith, a prophecy
Of bloom and fruitfulness to be.

Alfred Kummer, 1909

Above, El Camino Real through San Mateo, San Mateo County, c.1890, Carleton Watkins.
Left, Highland Place, Altadena, Los Angeles County, c.1900.

TODAY is ours, this moment all we know,
So quaff the cup of joy kind fates bestow;
"To all we love" the toast, and vow with me
No draught more precious flows in Arcady!

Ella M. Sexton, 1912

Above, road in West Bishop, Inyo County, c.1890, Andrew Forbes.
Left, wedding party, Montague, Siskiyou County, c.1900.

LAND of Heart's desire,

Where beauty has no ebb, decay no flood,

But joy is wisdom, time an endless song.

William Butler Yeats, 1894

Above and left, pergola, Fleming residence, Pasadena, 1906, Frederick Martin.

THE MODERN world has accustomed itself to look
upon California as the land of great surprises, the fulfiller
of great prophecies, the achiever of great works; in short,
its conditions have made it possible for its people to become
known far and wide as the doers of big things.

Zachary Arnold, 1910

Above, Santa Ana, Orange County, c.1900, Frederick Martin.
Left, Gillespie residence, Montecito, Santa Barbara County, c.1910, Frederick Martin.

THE PROSPECT of building a California state highway from San Francisco to San Diego, following the line of El Camino Real, the old mission road, is being much discussed at present. The step that naturally will follow will be the continuation of this road from San Francisco to Siskiyou; and when all has been accomplished, as it ultimately will be, California will be the possessor of a King's highway about 1,500 miles in length, a great thoroughfare with which no other state in the Union can hope ever to vie.

A Great State Highway, 1904

Above, Pacific Coast Highway, Santa Cruz County, c.1919.
Left, El Camino Real at Cahuenga Pass, looking north, Los Angeles County, c.1890.

Hints on Fueling an Automobile.

A **FOLDING** steel foot-rule is certainly worth the twenty cents it costs. Garage mechanics are frightful sinners in the way they plunge greasy files or any old thing into the gas tank to see how much gasoline you need. Your steel rule is compact and portable. Don't allow anything else to be used. If you are an economical man you will learn to gauge your tank exactly, and will thus probably save anything from twenty-five cents to a dollar a day. A wise motorist knows how much gas he wants, and sees that he gets it.

Lloyd Osbourne, 1911

Above, Kaweah, Tulare County, c.1905, Lindley Eddy.
Left, motoring in the San Gabriel Valley, Los Angeles County, c.1910, Frederick Martin.

Iᴛ ɪs ɢʟᴏʀʏ enough to have been the first man to see
California [from the air.] *Mon Dieu!* You cannot imagine it. No one
may imagine California as it is until he has done as I have done today,
until he has soared above the highest trees and then swept along fifty
or a hundred miles while, with no bother about the road, he gorged
his eyes upon the most amazing mixture of lights, shadows, and colors
that God used in painting the earth. Unless you fly, you do not see
the real California any more than a worm sliding through the Louvre
on its stomach would be likely to see the Mona Lisa.

Aviator Louis Paulhan, 1912

Above, Corte Madera Creek, Larkspur, Marin County, c.1900.
Left, summit of Mt. Diablo, looking west, Contra Costa County, c.1910.

To My Car

Brown as a Brahmin is she
   Who yields to my desire;
And she has been with dreamers
   And filled her heart with fire.

No need for speech between us;
   She knows my happy hand,
She shares my longing for the road
   The sky, the open land!

We hear the green fields calling,
   We feel the glad winds blow;
O life, how beautiful you are!
   O earth, how young you grow!

Winifred Webb, 1914

Above, Linda Vista Road, Pasadena, Los Angeles County, 1908, Frederick Martin.
Left, Santa Cruz Mountains, Santa Cruz County, c.1913, Frederick Martin.

CALIFORNIA, epitome of the seething, fermenting West, is quivering with life, ambition, hope. In the sun-flooded valleys along the Western Sea new ideals are timidly opening their first blossoms, a new civilization is in the making, a civilization akin to the glory of ancient Greece. Not today, not in this generation will the flower of this new idealism break into full blossom. California in truth is the "Land of Tomorrow."

Walter V. Woehlke, 1912

Above, orchards, Riverside County, c.1900.
Left, land sales office, Riverbank, Stanislaus County, c.1908.

I WONDER, FRIENDS OF MINE, YOU who have in former years been in the beautiful valley with me, if now that summer days have come, your thoughts turn with mine to the beloved Yosemite. Gray old El Capitan still sets his granite bulk as pillar and gate-post over against Inspiration Point, unmoved and unmovable. So he has stood for ages and so he shall stand to the last syllable of recorded time. It is good to have something as big and solid and unchangeable as that as a mental base and meridian on which we can fix our mental fulcrum and move in the magic world of beauty that lies around it.

Charles S. Greene, 1905

Above, Mirror Lake at sunrise, Yosemite Valley, Mariposa County, 1908, Frederick Martin.
Left, El Capitan, Yosemite Valley, 1908, Frederick Martin.

So much to do that is not e'en begun,
So much to hope for that we cannot see,
So much to win, so many things to be.

Lewis Morris, 1902

Above, Beverly Drive, Beverly Hills, Los Angeles County, c.1918, Frederick Martin.
Left motorcyclists, Ventura County, c.1913.

A<small>H CALIFORNIA,</small> we who recreate

The beauty and the charm of long ago

Ask ourselves. "Was it more real, that state,

Than this gay captured dream our children know

Because our love remembers?"

Kathleen Norris, 1900

A. Lindy, Larkspur, Marin County, 1892.

INDEX

Foothill Boulevard near Pomona, Los Angeles County, c.1910, Frederick Martin.

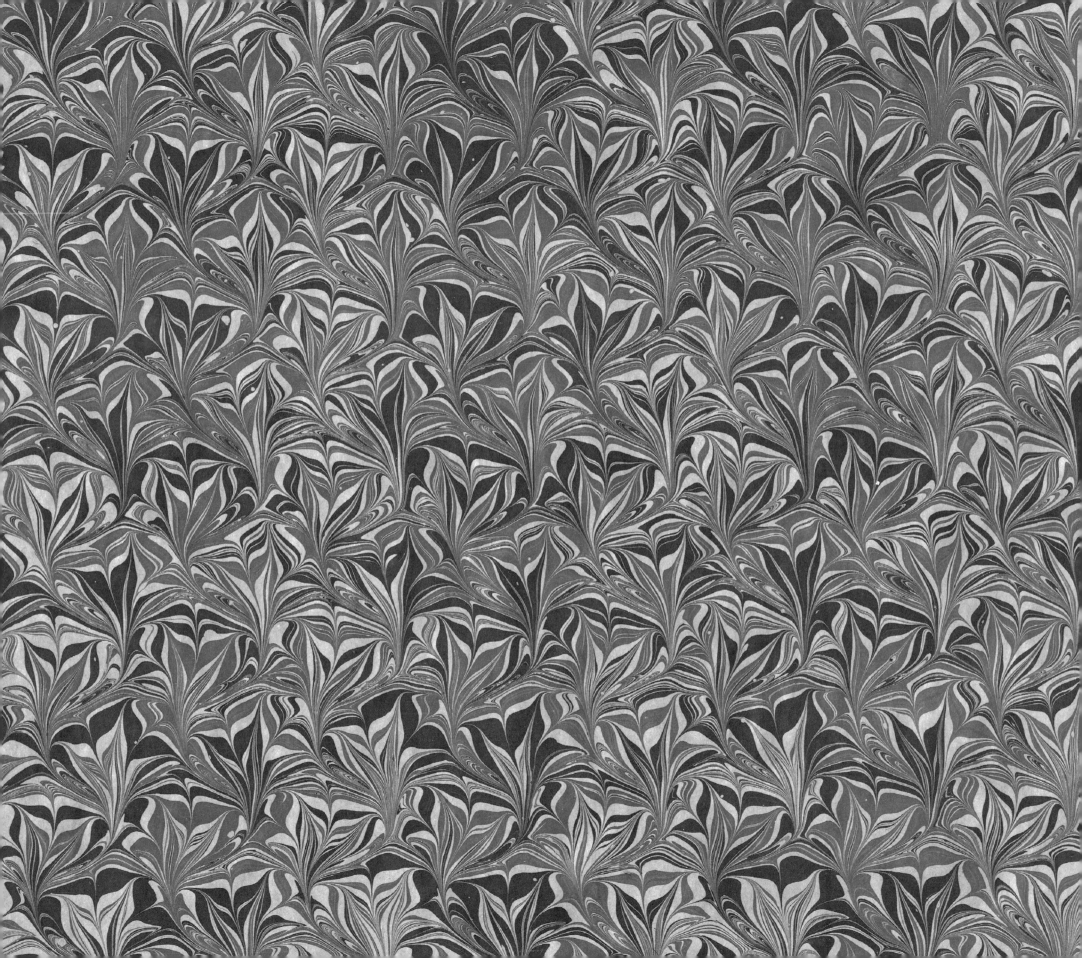